# The Bible With and Without Jesus:
# Leader Guide

# The Bible With and Without Jesus
## How Jews and Christians
## Read the Same Stories Differently

The Bible With and Without Jesus: Participant Guide

978-1-7910-3952-3

978-1-7910-3953-0 eBook

The Bible With and Without Jesus: DVD

978-1-7910-3956-1

The Bible With and Without Jesus: Leader Guide

978-1-7910-3954-7

978-1-7910-3955-4 eBook

# THE BIBLE WITH AND WITHOUT JESUS

## HOW JEWS AND CHRISTIANS
## READ THE SAME STORIES
## DIFFERENTLY

AMY-JILL LEVINE
MARC ZVI BRETTLER

ABINGDON PRESS | NASHVILLE

**The Bible With and Without Jesus**
How Jews and Christians Read the Same Stories Differently
Leader Guide

Copyright © 2025 Abingdon Press
All rights reserved.

978-1-7910-3954-7

MANUFACTURED IN THE UNITED STATES OF AMERICA

# CONTENTS

# Download a
# **FREE GLOSSARY**
## of terms used in this study .

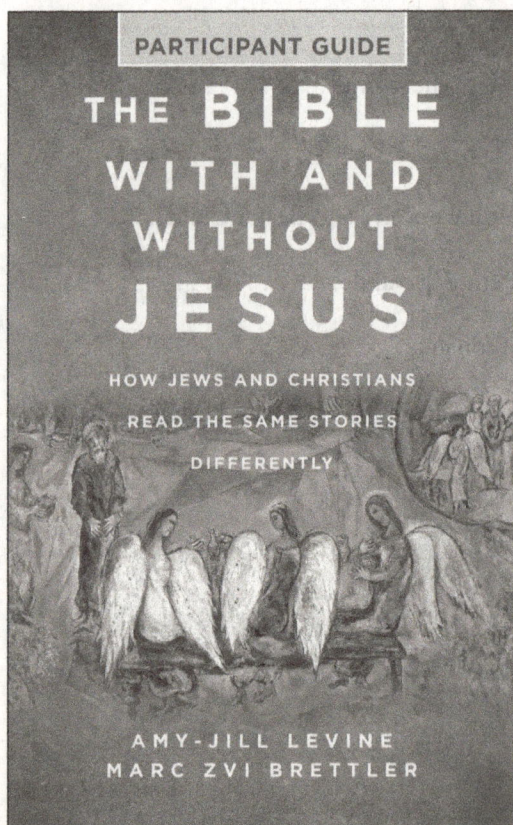

# INTRODUCTION

In their book *The Bible With and Without Jesus: How Jews and Christians Read the Same Stories Differently* (*BWWJ* in this Leader Guide), Amy-Jill (AJ) Levine and Marc Zvi Brettler address "texts from ancient Israel that are central in the New Testament" (5)[1] and discuss how passages Jews and Christians hold in common came to be read in different ways. Their goal is not to harmonize alternative readings between or even within Judaism and Christianity; nor is it to declare some interpretations "wrong" and others "right." Rather, AJ and Marc seek "to foster a different future" from a frequently contentious and polemical past, a future in which "Jews and Christians come to understand each other's positions and beliefs, and at the minimum, respectfully agree to disagree" (4).

This Leader Guide is designed to give adult students a model for studying *The Bible With and Without Jesus*. Although the primary audience for Abingdon Guides is Christian, this Guide envisions groups, whether of Christians, of Jews, or of Jews and Christians together, reading together several of the texts AJ and Marc highlight, perhaps alongside (selections from) several chapters of *The Bible With and Without Jesus,* then together talking about how and why different communities, over time, interpret those texts in different ways. It also envisions these conversations leading participants to take concrete actions based on what they learn, actions that help them love God and neighbor (Leviticus 19:18; Deuteronomy 6:5; Mark 12:31).

Leaders can best prepare for a successful study by reading chapters 3, 4, 8, 10, and 11 of *The Bible With and Without Jesus*, as these chapters form the basis of this study's sessions. As time permits, you will also want to read chapter 1 and the conclusion for a fuller understanding of AJ and Marc's

---

1 Throughout this leader guide, numbers in parentheses without any other notations refer to page numbers in *The Bible With and Without Jesus*.

goals. You will also want to review the accompanying Participant Guide, which summarizes the relevant chapters of *The Bible With and Without Jesus*.

Over the course of this study, you will invite participants to reconsider these texts:

### Session 1: The Creation of the World (BWWJ, chapter 3)

This session looks at Genesis 1, in which God not only creates an ordered world out of primordial chaos but also creates humanity in the divine image. We will explore some of the different ways that Jewish and Christian thinkers have made sense of this narrative and how these interpretations fit into their understandings of God and creation.

### Session 2: Adam and Eve (BWWJ, chapter 4)

Genesis 2–3 presents a different creation story. In this account, the first man and woman in the garden of Eden experience, depending on your perspective, either the Jewish "original opportunity" or the Christian "original sin." Questions to be considered include: What does the woman do to "help" the man? How does and should this narrative inform relationships between women and men today? What questions does it raise about our responsibility to "till…and keep" (Genesis 2:15) God's world? What does Genesis 2–3 suggest about justice and mercy?

### Session 3: "A Virgin Will Conceive and Bear a Child" (BWWJ, chapter 8)

Matthew, reading the Greek translation of Isaiah, sees a prophecy of a miraculous conception. Jews, reading Isaiah's original Hebrew, find a reference not to a virgin but to a pregnant young woman. This session situates Isaiah's prophecy of "Immanuel" (Hebrew for "God is with us") in its original historical context and shows how, for Isaiah and his immediate listeners, the sign of the pregnant woman relates to local politics. We then turn to problems and possibilities introduced when the Hebrew text is translated into Greek, and we conclude by considering the nature of signs, in biblical times and our own.

### *Session 4: Isaiah's Suffering Servant (BWWJ, chapter 9)*

Isaiah 52:13–53:12, the fourth of four servant songs in Isaiah, profoundly shapes how early Christians understood Jesus's life and death. For several Jewish interpreters, the text yields insights into the suffering of the people of Israel. Yet other meanings emerged for the people hearing this prophecy in its original context during the Babylonian Exile and then throughout history. How might the suffering servant help us perceive and respond to unjust suffering today?

### *Session 5: The Sign of Jonah (BWWJ, chapter 10)*

Often remembered only for a "whale" (though the book mentions only a "big fish"), Jonah is one of the Bible's most entertaining as well as ethically provocative stories. This session will examine Israel's most reluctant and successful prophet, consider how Jesus refers to the sign of Jonah, and look at how other interpreters, Jewish and Christian, have understood the book. Throughout, the discussion explores how this story confronts us with questions about sin and repentance, punishment and mercy, and who we believe God to be.

### *Session 6: "My God, My God, Why Have You Forsaken Me?" (BWWJ, chapter 11)*

No psalm has had a deeper impact on Christianity than Psalm 22. But while Christians generally read it as predicting Jesus's crucifixion, Jewish interpreters connect it with Queen Esther, King David, and a messianic figure other than Jesus. This session invites participants to reconsider this psalm of lament on its own terms and to explore the role of lament in their own relationship to God.

Each session plan in this Leader Guide contains the following:

- **Session Goals** to help you focus on outcomes most relevant and helpful to your group.
- **Biblical Foundations** are the main Scripture texts in each session, printed from the New Revised Standard Version (Updated Edition)

without verse numbers to support reading each passage as a whole unit. The Participant Guide notes verses where they are relevant to the discussion.

- **Before Your Session**—basic preparations.
- **Starting Your Session**—ideas for either "icebreaker" conversations or activities to "prime the pump," or both
- **Discussion Questions**—You will likely not have time to use all questions provided. Choose and use them to guide and shape a lively, constructive discussion.
- **Opening and Closing Prayers**—Because this Leader Guide envisions the possibility of Jews and Christians studying together, the prayers do not mention Jesus. Christian groups may wish to include specific references to Jesus in additional or augmented prayers. Participants may want to include new comments or substitute their own prayers or good wishes.

Thank you for leading your group in this study! May you find this Leader Guide informative and helpful as you facilitate your group's deeper engagement with and understanding of biblical texts that matter to both Judaism and Christianity, and for members of these traditions to continue to have positive relationships with each other and the world.

# SESSION 1

## The Creation of the World

### Session Goals

This session's readings, discussion, and reflection will help participants:

- understand some of the main differences between Jewish and Christian Bibles;
- appreciate how Genesis 1 emphasizes God's creative activity as bringing order to chaos;
- explore several Jewish and Christian ideas about whether and how other heavenly figures participated in Creation, and what these traditions mean for life today;
- consider how the equal creation of male and female, both in the divine image, may inform relationships between men and women and understandings of the human body; and
- identify ways they can engage constructively with God's ordered and good creation.

### Biblical Foundations

*When God began to create the heavens and the earth, the earth was complete chaos, and darkness covered the face of the deep, while a wind from God swept over the face of the waters. Then God said, "Let there be light," and there was light. And God saw that the light was good, and God separated the light from the darkness. God called the light Day, and the darkness he called Night. And there was evening and there was morning, the first day.*

*Genesis 1:1-5*

*Then God said, "Let us make humans in our image, according to our likeness, and let them have dominion over the fish of the sea and over the birds of the air and over the cattle and over all the wild animals of the earth and over every creeping thing that creeps upon the earth."*

*So God created humans in his image,*
*in the image of God he created them;*
*male and female he created them.*

*Genesis 1:26-27*

*In the beginning was the Word, and the Word was with God, and the Word was God. He was in the beginning with God. All things came into being through him, and without him not one thing came into being. What has come into being in him was life, and the life was the light of all people. The light shines in the darkness, and the darkness did not overtake it.*

*John 1:1-5*

## Before Your Session

- Carefully read, and reread, this session's Biblical Foundations. Note words and phrases—especially repeated words and phrases—that attract your attention, and think about what they might mean to you or to others in your group. Write down your questions and try to answer them. You may want to consult trusted Bible commentaries.

- Carefully read chapter 3 of *The Bible With and Without Jesus* (and, as preparation time allows, chapter 1). Review the summary for session 1 in the Participant Guide. Note topics about which you want to know more; you may want to consult reputable sources for further information.

- You will need either Bibles for in-person participants or slides with Scripture texts (identify the translation), or both; newsprint or markerboard and markers (for in-person sessions); paper, pens or pencils (in-person). Optional: Bibles from different Jewish and Christian traditions. (You might check with local libraries, bookstores, friends and neighbors, or clergy; https://www.biblegateway.com/ is also an excellent resource for many Bible translations.)

- If using the DVD or streaming video, preview session 1. Choose the best time in your session plan for viewing.

## Starting Your Session

Welcome participants. Briefly explain why you are excited to lead this study of *The Bible With and Without Jesus*. Invite volunteers to discuss their religious background and their familiarity with the Bible, and to talk briefly about what they want to gain from this class.

Ask for a show of hands indicating agreement or disagreement with these statements (please note that there is no "right" answer):

- The Bible is difficult to understand.
- The Bible is boring.
- The best way to know a biblical passage's meaning is to stick as closely as possible to its "plain sense."
- The Bible is God's Word.
- The Bible speaks to people today.
- People tend to quote the passages that they like.

Tell participants that, as they likely realize, each of these statements can and does provoke agreement and disagreement—between and, sometimes, even within communities, illustrating how the Bible is, as AJ and Marc write, "a contested work" (4).

Discuss:

- What are some of the biggest differences you've encountered in how people read the Bible?
- Why do you think people interpret the same Bible passage in different ways?
- How can understanding different ways people read the Bible help us better understand one another, and ourselves? How can it help us better understand the Bible's importance?

Tell participants *The Bible With and Without Jesus* focuses on different ways Jews and Christians read "texts from ancient Israel that are central in

13

the New Testament" (5). Acknowledge neither all Jews nor all Christians read the Bible the same way. AJ and Marc's book explores major historical interpretive issues that matter within and between Jewish and Christian traditions today, but it by no means covers all Jewish and Christian biblical interpretation.

## Opening Prayer

*Most Holy One, you are the God who speaks. In the sacred writings, you challenge and comfort, reprimand and reassure, and illuminate the way of life. In this study, guide us more fully to receive and respond to you—through Scripture, through our conversations with one another, and through acts of loving-kindness. Amen.*

## Watch the Session 1 Video

Discuss:

- What statements in this video most interested, intrigued, surprised, or confused you? Why?
- What questions does this video raise for you?

## Christian and Jewish Bibles

Have participants locate these books in their Bibles:

- Genesis
- Revelation (and note that the correct title is Revelation, not Revelations)
- Psalm 23
- Psalm 151
- Joshua
- John
- Ecclesiasticus (*not* Ecclesiastes)
- Obadiah

- 2 Corinthians
- Tobit

To find all these books, participants will need Bibles containing not only the Tanakh/Old Testament but also both the Deuterocanonical Books/Old Testament Apocrypha and the New Testament. Use this activity to illustrate, as AJ and Marc write, "the Bible, in the singular, does not exist; different communities have different Bibles" (3). Only some Eastern Orthodox Bibles include Psalm 151. Only Roman Catholic, Anglican, and Eastern Orthodox Bibles include Ecclesiasticus (or the Wisdom of [Jesus ben] Sirach), and Tobit. No Jewish Bible includes any book from the Deuterocanonical collection or the New Testament.

Communicate these points in a mini-lecture:

- The word *Bible* means "books" (Greek, *biblia*) and suggests a collection of books a community regards as authoritative—that is, a *canon.*
- The Jewish canon has been known since the Middle Ages as the Tanakh, an acronym for these three parts of Scripture:
  ◊ *Torah* ("Instruction": the first five books—also known as the Pentateuch, sometimes misleadingly called the Law)
  ◊ *Nevi'im* ("Prophets": Joshua and Judges; 1, 2 Samuel; 1, 2 Kings; Isaiah; Jeremiah; Ezekiel; and the twelve "minor" prophets, such as Amos, Hosea, and Micah)
  ◊ *Ketuvim* ("Writings," including Psalms and Proverbs, Ruth, Esther, 1 and 2 Chronicles).
- The Christian Bible has two parts, the Old Testament and the New Testament. "Old" does not mean outdated; it means foundational, bedrock. The Tanakh and the Protestant Old Testament contain the same books but order them differently, so Tanakh and Old Testament are not synonymous. The Jewish ordering emphasizes the centrality of the land of Israel; the Tanakh's last book is 2 Chronicles, which ends with King Cyrus of Persia repatriating the exiled Judeans in Babylon to their national homeland. The

Christian Old Testament ordering, emphasizing prophecy and its fulfillment in Jesus, ends with the Book of Malachi, which predicts the return of the prophet Elijah to announce the messianic age.

- Not all Christians share the same Old Testament. Roman Catholic, Anglican, and Eastern Orthodox communities include the Apocrypha or Deuterocanonical books, Jewish books written in or at least preserved in Greek before the New Testament and not part of the Jewish or Protestant canons.
- Most of the Jewish canon was originally written in Hebrew, with small portions written in Aramaic. All New Testament books were originally written in Greek. While Roman Catholics and Protestants regard the Hebrew of the Old Testament as authoritative, many Eastern Orthodox churches, such as the Greek Orthodox Church, consider the Greek translation of the Hebrew texts (the Septuagint) to be authoritative.

Discuss:

- How much experience, if any, have you had with Bibles other than the Bible with which you are most familiar?
- How do you think the reality of different Bibles, and different translations, affects conversations about "what the Bible says"? Can you provide any examples?
- Do you think people should learn either Greek or Hebrew, or both, to understand the Bible, or are you comfortable with English translations? Do you think of the King James Version as the "authorized" text?

*Optional*: If you have gathered Bibles from different traditions, pass them around for participants to compare and contrast.

## Making Order from Chaos

Have participants turn in their Bibles to Genesis 1. Recruit a volunteer to read aloud 1:1-5. If possible, recruit a second volunteer to read the same verses aloud in a different translation and have participants note variations.

Remind participants these verses begin the first of two Creation stories in Genesis. This story is from the Priestly source (P), one of several literarily identifiable sources in the Torah.

Discuss:

- AJ and Marc say Genesis 1:1 "is one of the Bible's most discussed, most mistranslated, and therefore most misunderstood texts" (75–76). What difference does reading the verse as an independent sentence ("In the beginning God created") or an introductory clause ("When God began to create") make?
- How does the idea that verse 1 describes bringing order from chaos instead of creating out of nothing (*ex nihilo*) affect your ideas about God as Creator?
- In each day of Creation, God brings order by separating light from darkness, water from land, varieties of plants and animals, the Sabbath from other days of the week. What picture of the natural world does this story paint? How much does it align with your understanding of how the world came into being or how it now functions?
- How can we continue to participate in God's creative activity by bringing order to chaos? How do we know when our efforts oppose rather than align with God's work?

## Wind, Spirit, Wisdom, *Logos*

Discuss:

- The Hebrew word *ru'ach* in Genesis 1:2 can be translated "wind," "breath," or "spirit." What does each translation bring to your image of God's creative activity? What does your translation choose?
- Marc and AJ note, "In the Tanakh, the spirit is something God has, or can bestow"—for example, Isaiah 11:2 ("the spirit of the LORD shall rest on him, the spirit of wisdom and understanding, the spirit of counsel and might, the spirit of knowledge and the fear of

the LORD"), "but it is not a deity, an angel, an object of worship, or what in some Christian teachings is called a 'person'" (78). While Christians traditionally see the *ru'ach 'elohim* in Genesis 1:2 as the Holy Spirit (so the King James Version's "And the Spirit of God moved upon the face of the waters"), Jews do not. How do you understand the "Holy Spirit"?

- Because *ru'ach* is a grammatically feminine noun, it came to be associated with Wisdom, sometimes depicted as a separate, divine, female figure closely connected to God (the Greek word for "wisdom" is *sophia*). How do you understand Proverbs 8:22-36, which depicts Wisdom's role in creation? What does Wisdom's role in creation mean for human life?

- Baruch (a Jewish text from the second or third century before Jesus) says Wisdom "appeared on earth and lived with humankind" as "the book of the commandments of God" (3:38; 4:1). "For the rabbis, Wisdom…was identical to the Torah" (84). What does this claim suggest about the importance of the Torah within the Jewish tradition? Do we see the Christ as having the same, or a similar role in Christianity?

- Later rabbinic Judaism associated the *ru'ach* with the glory of God, especially the *Shekhinah*, God's female aspect in later Jewish mysticism; see also the cloud indicating God's presence at the Tabernacle in Exodus 40:34-38. When and how would you say you've seen God's glory? Did it seem to you to be gendered?

- Read Psalm 33:6-9. How is its description of God's creative activity like and unlike those in Genesis 1 and Proverbs 8? What implications does God's creative speech have for how humans ought to speak? Do you find that words can be powerful? Are there any words that have "stayed with you" or guided you?

- The first-century Jewish philosopher Philo of Alexandria wrote about God's word (Greek *logos*) as an "archangel" and as the child of God and Wisdom who mediates between God and humanity: pleading to God on mortals' behalf, pledging both that humanity will never entirely choose chaos and that God will not overlook the created world (see 86). How do you understand the divine "word" and its relationship to "hearing"?

- John 1:1-5 identifies the Word both as God and with God. How do you understand this relationship?
- In what ways do words "create"? In what ways do we "hear" God?

## "Let Us Make Humankind..."

Recruit a volunteer to read aloud Genesis 1:26-27. Discuss:

- Why do you think God might have consulted with the divine council before creating humanity? What implications might God's consultation have for how we exercise authority?
- Although God's proposal to create humanity is in the plural, "the next verse refers to God three times, *always in the singular*, to describe this creation" (91). What is the significance of God acting alone to create human beings?
- The Hebrew words for "image" and "likeness" in verse 27 "almost always refer to physical appearances" (91). How do you understand the idea that people are in the divine image? What would it mean to see the divine image in people we dislike? Does being in the divine image mean, as Jewish sources teach, that one should be merciful as God is merciful, or compassionate as God is compassionate?
- Christians often see God's plural speech as indicating the Trinity (the Christian belief that God exists in three manifestations or "persons"). AJ and Marc find this idea "theologically understandable" but based on their study of the Hebrew of Genesis 1:26 and its original context, "historically untenable" (92). How do you understand the Trinity?
- Later Jewish traditions identify the others to whom God speaks in various ways—often the angelic hosts, but also God's other created works, God's own heart, righteous preexistent souls, Wisdom, the preexistent Torah—and several interpretations suggest God created humanity over objections from others (for details, see 93–97). Some of these options would also be "theologically understandable

but historically untenable." What does this mean? What claims about God and God's relationship to humanity do such traditions make? What insights do they offer today?

## Call to Action

Read aloud from *The Bible With and Without Jesus,* (98)*:* "We hope that our readers will look beyond these fraught verses [in Genesis 1] and read the first creation story as a whole—a marvelously structured story that makes a strong claim for an ordered, good world, in which people can play a central and constructive role."

Ask participants to identify projects or causes in which they are involved or with which they are familiar that engage constructively with God's ordered and originally "very good" (see Genesis 1:31) creation. Choose some way your group can support one or more of these projects.

## Closing Prayer

*O God, when two people study your Word, your glory is present. May your presence continue to abide with us as we go out into the good world you have made. Show us where and how we can reflect your wisdom, generosity, and love, as your living images. Amen.*

# SESSION 2

## Adam and Eve

### Session Goals

This session's readings, discussion, and reflection will help participants:

- understand why scholars understand Genesis 1:1–2:4a (in shorthand: Genesis 1) and 2:4b–3:24 (in shorthand: Genesis 2–3) as two distinct stories;
- consider the relationship between the man and the woman before and after they ate the fruit, and the implications of those relationships for women and men today;
- determine whether Genesis 3 warrants typical conclusions about women's roles, human sexuality, and sin, especially the idea of original sin (that because of events in Eden, all people inherit a sinful state);
- consider questions Genesis 2–3 raises about ecology, and how you might understand them in light of Genesis 1; and
- consider whether Genesis 1–3 should be taught in public schools and if so, how?

### Biblical Foundations

*In the day that the LORD God made the earth and the heavens, when no plant of the field was yet in the earth and no vegetation of the field had yet sprung up—for the LORD God had not caused it to rain upon the earth, and there was no one to till the ground, but a stream would rise from the earth and water the whole face of the ground—then the LORD God formed man from the dust of the ground and breathed into his nostrils the breath of life, and the man became a living being. And the LORD God planted a garden in Eden, in* the east, and there he put the man whom he had formed. Out of the ground the LORD God made to grow every tree that is pleasant to the sight and good for food, the tree of life also in the midst of the garden, and the tree of the knowledge of good and evil.

*Genesis 2:4b-9*

Then the LORD God said, "It is not good that the man should be alone; I will make him a helper as his partner."...So the LORD God caused a deep sleep to fall upon the man, and he slept; then he took one of his ribs and closed up its place with flesh. And the rib that the LORD God had taken from the man he made into a woman and brought her to the man. Then the man said,

> "This at last is bone of my bones
>         and flesh of my flesh;
> this one shall be called Woman,
>         for out of Man this one was taken."

*Genesis 2:18, 21-23*

To the woman [the LORD God] said,
>         "I will make your pangs in childbirth exceedingly great;
>                 in pain you shall bring forth children,
>         yet your desire shall be for your husband,
>                 and he shall rule over you."
And to the man [the LORD God] said,
>         "Because you have listened to the voice of your wife
>                 and have eaten of the tree
>         about which I commanded you,
>                 'You shall not eat of it,'
>         cursed is the ground because of you;
>                 in toil you shall eat of it all the days of your life;
>         thorns and thistles it shall bring forth for you;
>                 and you shall eat the plants of the field.
>         By the sweat of your face
>                 you shall eat bread
>         until you return to the ground,
>                 for out of it you were taken;
>         you are dust,
>                 and to dust you shall return."

*Genesis 3:16-19*

# Before Your Session

- Carefully read and reread this session's Biblical Foundations. Note words and phrases that attract your attention, and think about what they might mean to you or to others in your group.
- Consider why scholars understand Genesis 1:1–2:4a and 2:4b–3:24 as two distinct stories.
- Write down your questions and try to answer them; you may want to consult trusted Bible commentaries.
- Carefully read chapter 4 of *The Bible With and Without Jesus*. Review the summary for session 2 in the Participant Guide. Note topics about which you want to know more; you may want to consult reputable sources for further information.
- You will need either Bibles for in-person participants or slides prepared with Scripture texts (identify the translation), or both; newsprint or a markerboard and markers (for in-person sessions); paper, pens or pencils (in-person).
- If using the DVD or streaming video, preview session 2. Choose the best time in your session plan for viewing.
- Optional: Gather examples of visual art depicting Genesis 2–3. Choose pieces from a variety of time periods, sources (religious and otherwise), and cultures. You may also want to consider art directed to children. Describe the extent to which this art accurately follows the biblical text, and consider what details absent in the text the art fills in (e.g., what the first man and woman look like).

# Starting Your Session

Welcome participants. Lead participants in brainstorming a list of everything they know or think they know about the story of the garden of Eden. Write responses on newsprint or markerboard.

*Optional*: Display the artwork you collected. Invite participants to determine which artistic renditions appeal to them most and least, and why. What details in them, if any, do they think go beyond the Bible's story? What new insights into or questions about the story does the art prompt?

Ask participants how they understand the term *myth*, if they think the term reflects a negative value judgment and if it might be appropriate for the Bible. Introduce this definition of *myth* from *The Bible With and Without Jesus*: "a metaphorical tale designed to explain why life is the way it is" (105). Read aloud from *The Bible With and Without Jesus* (133): "The story of Eden is a myth of how things came to be. It is not, however, a prescription for how things must be. Instead, it prompts us to ask the necessary questions about how things *should* be." Tell participants your group will ask such questions in its study of Genesis 2–3.

## Opening Prayer

*Creator God, in your wisdom and goodness you did not make us to be alone. We approach you as a community you have called together to hear, discern, and do your will. As we read this ancient story, renew our commitment to living faithfully and to nurturing your gift of life. Amen.*

## Watch Session Video

Watch the session 2 video segment together. Discuss:

- What statements in this video segment most interested, intrigued, surprised, or confused you? Why?
- What questions does this video segment raise for you?

## The Garden of Eden

Tell participants Genesis 2:4b–3:24 is the second of the two creation stories in Genesis. It is from the Yawhist source in the Torah/Pentateuch because it uses the Hebrew consonants YHWH as its primary name for God, while the Priestly source uses "Elohim." (Note: YHWH can be pronounced "Yahweh," although observant Jews substitute "Adonai" [Hebrew, "my Lord"]; most English translations offer "Lord." Late nineteenth-century

German biblical scholarship gives the source its abbreviation, J for Jahwe, the equivalent of the English YHWH.)

Recruit a volunteer to read aloud Genesis 2:4b-9. Discuss:

- How does the order of Creation in Genesis 2 differ from Genesis 1? What significance, if any, do you find in these differences?

- In Hebrew, the "man" God forms from the dust (verse 7) is *ha'adam*—not the proper name "Adam" (which doesn't appear until 4:25) but "the earthling," since the word is a pun on *'adamah* (Hebrew for "earth" or "ground"). What significance, if any, do you find in the idea that the human being is created from the soil? Do you think of God as a potter (see Isaiah 64:8; Jeremiah 18:16; Sirach 33:13) and if so, what does this image suggest about human bodies and the divine-human relationship?

- The "breath of life" God breathes into the earthling's nostrils (verse 7) is the "life force," "self," "inner life," or "very being" (107); later interpreters often understood this force as the "soul" understood to be eternal, although the Hebrew doesn't support that reading. Does the connection of God to this breath that animates us make you think any differently about inhaling and exhaling?

- How does knowing the name *Eden* likely derives from a Hebrew root meaning "bliss" and "pleasure" affect your image of the garden? If you could construct your own place of "bliss" or "pleasure," what would it look like? What would you do in it? Who would be with you, since according to Genesis 2:18 it is not good for the human being to be alone?

- "The (probably) first-century Jewish author known as Pseudo-Philo suggests that the garden has been preserved and will be inherited by the resurrected righteous" (107). New Testament references to "Paradise" (for example, Luke 23:43; Revelation 2:7) may suggest Eden. How much are your own ideas about and images of the afterlife like or unlike the garden of Eden? Why?

- AJ and Marc point out that the four rivers Genesis 2:10 states flow from Eden do not meet and never have. What do we lose or gain, or both, by thinking of the garden of Eden as "everywhere and nowhere" (108)?

- How do you understand the earthling's role in the garden? Is its task—"to till it and keep it" (Genesis 2:15)—relevant for us today?
- Why do you think God warns the earthling about eating fruit from the tree of the knowledge of good and evil? Do you think God wants the first humans to assert free will and leave the garden? Does reading Genesis 2 in light of Genesis 1:28 ("fill the earth") change your understanding of God's command regarding the fruit?
- Recruit a volunteer to read aloud Genesis 2:18-23. Discuss:
- The Bible speaks of God as a "helper" (Hebrew *ezer*; see for example, Genesis 49:25; Exodus 18:4; Deuteronomy 33:7). In what ways do "partners" and "God" help each other?
- Why do you think God make multiple attempts to create the earthling's partner (Genesis 2:19-23)? What conclusions might you draw from the fact that God's first experiment to find a suitable match for the human being fails? What conclusions might you draw from this story about our relationship to "every animal of the field and every bird of the air"?
- What makes the newly created being an appropriate helper and partner for the earthling? What does the newly created being do to help?
- Some early interpreters (like Philo; see also 1 Corinthians 11:7-12; 1 Timothy 2:11-15) argue the woman's creation from the man's rib (or side) means men are superior to and have authority over women. Do you think Genesis 2 supports that hierarchy? Why or why not?

## Eating Forbidden Fruit

Recruit volunteers to read aloud Genesis 3, taking the roles of the narrator, the snake, the woman, the man, and God. Discuss:

- AJ and Marc note the description of the snake is the only instance of "crafty" being a negative trait in the Tanakh (contrast

Proverbs 13:16 where the same Hebrew word is translated "clever"; the same term, in Greek, appears in Matthew 10:16 [the NRSVue translates it here as "wise"] and in Luke 16:8 [the NRSVue translates it here as "shrewd"]). Do you see "crafty," "clever," and "wise" as synonymous? Are these traits you would like to possess or for which you would like to be known?

- The story doesn't reveal why the snake talks with the woman. What do you think motivated the snake? Later texts (e.g., 2 Corinthians 11:3; Revelation 20:2) suggest that the snake was the devil. Does this interpretation change your understanding of the events in the garden?

- How do you assess the woman's action: was it a considered, intelligent decision, or a transgression and an overstepping of her role (see 113–114)? To what extent, if any, does your conclusion depend on who told the woman that the fruit was forbidden?

- "The type of knowledge the tree of the knowledge of good and evil provides is ultimate, sexual knowledge" (114–115). How would you characterize this story's attitude toward sexuality?

- What consequences do the snake, the woman, the man, and the earth face for the humans' eating of the forbidden fruit (verses 14-19)? With which of these is the word *curse* used? To what extent do you believe these consequences are appropriate?

- Do you think God exiles the man and woman from Eden as punishment, in mercy, both, or neither? Why? Do you see this story as the "fall" of humanity? If so, from what have we fallen?

## Concerning Original Sin

- The word *sin* is absent from Genesis 2–3 (118). How do you define "sin"? How does your definition determine whether or not you read the story of Eden as a story about sin?

- Augustine interpreted the story to mean "all people, as descendants of Adam, are born with the taint of this 'original sin' and so are guilty and deserving of damnation—an idea found neither in the

Hebrew nor the Greek versions of Genesis" (101). Why do you think this idea developed? How do you understand original sin? Is the concept either helpful or harmful, or both, and how?

- Rabbinic literature teaches obedience to God's covenant is the antidote to sin: "Jews do not follow the Torah to 'earn' divine love. Jews lovingly follow the Torah in response to the love God showed Israel by giving the Torah to them" (129). What motivates you to "do the right thing": love of God, recognizing everyone in the divine image, fear of arrest, avoidance of guilt or shame, fear of hell, or something else?

- The late first-century text 2 Baruch, states, "Each of us has been the Adam of his own soul" (54:19) (see 126–127). Some biblical texts recognize generational guilt (Exodus 20:5; Deuteronomy 5:9), while others challenge the idea (Deuteronomy 7:9-10; Jeremiah 31:29-30; Ezekiel 18:1-4). In what sense does each generation suffer for its own sins? In what sense do generations pay and even die for the sins of their forebears?

## Call to Action

Remind participants that AJ and Marc read Genesis 2–3 as a mythic description of how things *came* to be, not a binding prescription for how things *must* be.

Ask participants to identify priorities they think people who value this story should pursue related to one or more of the following issues the story raises:

- How we treat God's created world (earth, plants, animals).
- How we understand "sin" and what can be done to prevent it.
- How this story should be taught to others, especially children: as myth, science, one of multiple Creation narratives, the "way things happened"?
- How does your understanding of Jesus impact, if at all, your understanding of Genesis 2–3?

## Closing Prayer

*From the dust, O God, you formed us for one another and for you. Though our first parents tried to hide from you, you do not hide yourself from us. You continue to walk with us outside the garden, empowering us to fulfill the calling you gave. May we live as faithful stewards of the earth, helpers and partners to one another, and participants in your creativity and compassion. Amen.*

# SESSION 3

# "A Virgin Will Conceive and Bear a Child"

## Session Goals

This session's readings, discussion, and reflection will help participants:

- understand the historical context in which Isaiah announced the sign of Immanuel;
- explain how and why Matthew uses Isaiah's prophecy to describe Mary's virginal conception;
- appreciate that there is no single biblical text;
- appreciate how and why different traditions read Isaiah's prophecy differently; and
- reflect on the nature of signs and their interpretations, including what might be considered "signs" today.

## Biblical Foundations

*Again the LORD spoke to Ahaz, saying, "Ask a sign of the LORD your God; let it be deep as Sheol or high as heaven." But Ahaz said, "I will not ask, and I will not put the LORD to the test." Then Isaiah said, "Hear then, O house of David! Is it too little for you to weary mortals that you weary my God also? Therefore the Lord himself will give you a sign. Look, the young woman is with child and shall bear a son and shall name him Immanuel. He shall eat curds and honey by the time he knows how to refuse the evil and choose the good. For before the child knows how to refuse the evil and choose the good, the land before whose two kings you are in dread will be deserted."*

*Isaiah 7:10-16*

*Now the birth of Jesus the Messiah took place in this way. When his mother Mary had been engaged to Joseph, but before they lived together, she was found to be pregnant from the Holy Spirit. Her husband Joseph, being a righteous man and unwilling to expose her to public disgrace, planned to divorce her quietly. But just when he had resolved to do this, an angel of the Lord appeared to him in a dream and said, "Joseph, son of David, do not be afraid to take Mary as your wife, for the child conceived in her is from the Holy Spirit. She will bear a son, and you are to name him Jesus, for he will save his people from their sins." All this took place to fulfill what had been spoken by the Lord through the prophet:*

*"Look, the virgin shall become pregnant and give birth to a son,*
*and they shall name him Emmanuel,"*

*which means, "God is with us." When Joseph awoke from sleep, he did as the angel of the Lord commanded him; he took her as his wife but had no marital relations with her until she had given birth to a son, and he named him Jesus.*

*Matthew 1:18-25*

## Before Your Session

- Carefully read and reread this session's Biblical Foundations. Note words and phrases that attract your attention, and think about what they might mean to you or to others in your group. Write down your questions and try to answer them; you may want to consult trusted Bible commentaries.
- Carefully read chapter 8 of *The Bible With and Without Jesus*. Review the summary for session 3 in the Participant Guide. Note topics about which you want to know more; you may want to consult reputable sources for further information.
- You will need either Bibles for in-person participants or slides prepared with Scripture texts for sharing (identify the translation), or both; newsprint or a markerboard and markers (for in-person sessions); paper, pens or pencils (in-person).
- If using the DVD or streaming video, preview session 3. Choose the best time in your session plan for viewing.

## Starting Your Session

Welcome participants. Find a piece of art that has had multiple interpretations (Da Vinci's *Mona Lisa* and *The Last Supper*; Bartholdi's *Statue of Liberty*; Michelangelo's *The Creation of Adam*; Grant Wood's *American Gothic*; Munch's *The Scream*, etc.). Ask the group to suggest what the painting "means" or if they can summarize it in one sentence (remind them that there is no right or wrong answer).

Ask them if, in interpreting a work of art, any of the following should matter: its date, where it was painted, the biography of the painter, its cost, what famous art critics have said about it, and so on.

Suggest that, as are many biblical verses, Isaiah 7:14 is like a painting that conveys different meanings to different audiences. This session will help participants understand why.

## Opening Prayer

*Sovereign God, you rule over both the miraculous and the mundane. Signs of your power and presence fill the world and our lives. May the Scripture we hear, discuss, and ponder today be such a sign for us. Amen.*

## Watch Session Video

Watch the session 3 video together. Discuss:

- What statements in this video most interested, intrigued, surprised, or confused you? Why?
- What questions does this video raise for you?

## Isaiah in His Context

Review these points with your participants (you may also wish to display or have participants refer to a map of the Middle East in Isaiah's time; you may want to consult trusted study Bibles or websites):

- According to the Bible, after the death of King Solomon in approximately 931 BCE, the nation of Israel split into two kingdoms when ten of the twelve tribes rejected the (unjust) rule of Solomon's son Rehoboam. One was the Northern Kingdom of Israel, whose capital eventually was Samaria, and which biblical prophets often called "Ephraim" after the dominant tribe. The other was the Southern Kingdom of Judah, after its dominant tribe, whose capital was Jerusalem.
- In the late eighth century, the Assyrian Empire, which encompassed much of modern Iraq and southeastern Turkey, was expanding.
- King Pekah of Israel (Northern Kingdom) and King Rezin of the city-state of Damascus (Aram) formed an alliance to resist Assyria, and they wanted King Ahaz of Judah to join them.
- Ahaz, thinking it safer, made Judah a vassal state of Assyria. The new alliance attempts to attack Jerusalem.

After reviewing the history, recruit a volunteer to read aloud Isaiah 7:1-9. Discuss:

- Why do you think Isaiah says, "The heart of Ahaz and the heart of his people shook as the trees of the forest shake before the wind" (Isaiah 7:2)?
- Why do you think Isaiah tells Ahaz that he should not be afraid?
- Do you think religion or people who represent religious groups should be involved in politics?

Recruit a volunteer to read aloud Isaiah 7:10-16. Discuss:

- Why do you think God tells Ahaz to ask for a sign? Why do you think Ahaz refuses?
- AJ and Marc cite several examples of biblical signs, including Genesis 17:11 (circumcision, the "sign of the covenant"); Exodus 7:3 (signs and wonders in Egypt, the ten plagues); Judges 6:36-40 (dew on fleece); 2 Kings 20:8-11 (behavior of a shadow); Isaiah 20:3 (Isaiah walks naked and barefoot for three years); Matthew 26:48

(the kiss Judas gives Jesus); Luke 2:12 (a child wrapped in cloths); John 2:11 (turning water into wine). How are these signs alike and different? To which of these signs is the sign of Isaiah 7 most similar? Do you know any other signs from Scripture? You can search for the word *sign* on https://www.biblegateway.com/ to find examples.

- If God invited—or commanded—you to ask for a sign, what sign would you ask for, and why? How do we tell if something is a "sign from God"? If someone told you of having received such a sign, how would you react: question, trust, doubt, smile, or something else?
- What sign does Isaiah say God will give Ahaz?
- The Hebrew name *Immanuel* means "with us is God." Does your name have symbolic value? Does that symbolism impact your sense of self?

## From "Young Woman" to "Virgin"

Discuss:

- The Hebrew of Isaiah 7:14 says "the young woman is with child" or "the young woman is pregnant." What if anything does pregnancy suggest to you? If you see a pregnant woman today, do any particular thoughts occur?
- The Septuagint (the Greek translation of the Hebrew text) uses *parthenos* in Isaiah 7:14. The Greek also says that she will be with child rather than that she is pregnant. *Parthenos* can connote virginity (though it need not do so). In your view, do these differences change the meaning of Isaiah's sign? Why or why not?

Recruit a volunteer to read aloud Matthew 1:18-25. Discuss:

- How does Matthew's use of the Greek version of Isaiah 7:14 present the sign as miraculous?

- Of the four New Testament Gospels, only Matthew and Luke discuss Jesus's conception and birth, and only Matthew explicitly presents it as miraculous (see 259). Why do you think Matthew includes notice of a virginal conception? Why do you think it is absent from the rest of the New Testament? To what extent does your understanding of Jesus, or his mother Mary, depend on this miraculous conception?

- Matthew uses Isaiah 7:14 as one of many "fulfillment citations" that connect events in Jesus's life with verses from Israel's Scriptures. Why do you think Matthew is concerned to show Jesus's connection to Israel's history?

- Matthew's use of "Immanuel" ("God is with us") in 1:23 balances Jesus's promise to his disciples at the Gospel's end, 28:20. What does this framing suggest to you? How, if at all, do you feel the presence of the divine?

- "Ascription of divine conception usually worked backward: a person of impressive prowess or intellect had to be the child of a god; nothing else would explain his (always 'his') extraordinary accomplishments" (273). How is Matthew's story of Jesus's divine conception like and unlike such stories (e.g., of Hercules, Theseus, Alexander the Great, Augustus Caesar) in the Greco-Roman world?

- "Divine conceptions also appear in Israel's Scriptures," as in stories about the "sons of God" producing a race of giants with the "daughters of men" (Genesis 6:2-4 KJV), or in the intimation in Judges 13 that Samson's mother "had some angelic help in conceiving her child" (273). To what extent, if any, do claims of divine conception matter to you? To what extent, if any, does virginity prior to marriage matter?

- Christian writers used Isaiah 7:14 as evidence of Mary's perpetual virginity, after Jesus's birth, though the Gospels and Paul's letters mention Jesus's siblings (see 259–260). Why do you think claims of Mary's perpetual virginity were important to some Christians and not to others? Do claims regarding Mary's virginity make Mary more, or less, a role model or relatable?

- "The issue is not one of right reading versus wrong reading; rather, if one begins with the premise that the Christ is predicted by and present in what becomes called the 'Old Testament,' one will find him there" (274). Have you had experiences where what is obvious to you is opaque to someone else? Do these differences complicate relationships? How might you overcome these difficulties?
- In Justin Martyr's *Dialogue with Trypho*, Trypho the Jew says to the Christian Justin, "If we could do this more frequently we should receive more benefit, while we examine the very words [of Scripture] themselves" (quoted on 277). Why is "examin[ing] the very words" important when reading Scripture? What benefits do we gain from reading Scripture with others, including those who hold interpretations different from the ones we hold?

## Call to Action

Read aloud from *The Bible With and Without Jesus*: "Too often today blind faith is emphasized. Yet all readings of [Isaiah 7] suggest that it is not only proper but on occasion crucial to doubt, to ask God to provide signs about future events. Isaiah speaks of a sign given to Ahaz, a king who refuses to believe the prophet's original message and refused to look for a sign: What are the signs given to people who refuse to believe the signs of the times?" (283).

Discuss:

- How would you define a "sign"?
- What are "the signs of the times" you are most concerned about, and why?
- How do and how can you live as a sign of God's presence in the world?
- What signs of God's activity catch your attention, and how do you respond?

## Closing Prayer

*Lord God, we ask that you make us living signs of your love for others. Amen.*

# SESSION 4

# Isaiah's Suffering Servant

## Session Goals

This session's readings, discussion, and reflection will help participants:

- understand how New Testament authors understood Jesus through Isaiah 52:13–53:12;
- examine Isaiah 52:13–53:12 in its original historical context;
- appreciate how Jewish and Christian interpreters understood, and understand, the identity of the servant in Isaiah 52:13–53:12; and
- identify ways to recognize and alleviate unjust suffering.

## Biblical Foundation

See, my servant shall prosper;
    he shall be exalted and lifted up
    and shall be very high.
Just as there were many who were astonished at him
    —so marred was his appearance, beyond human semblance,
    and his form beyond that of mortals—
so he shall startle many nations;
    kings shall shut their mouths because of him,
for that which had not been told them they shall see,
    and that which they had not heard they shall contemplate.

Who has believed what we have heard?
    And to whom has the arm of the LORD been revealed?
For he grew up before him like a young plant
    and like a root out of dry ground;
he had no form or majesty that we should look at him,
    nothing in his appearance that we should desire him.

He was despised and rejected by others;
      a man of suffering and acquainted with infirmity,
and as one from whom others hide their faces
      he was despised, and we held him of no account.

Surely he has borne our infirmities
      and carried our diseases,
yet we accounted him stricken,
      struck down by God, and afflicted.
But he was wounded for our transgressions,
      crushed for our iniquities;
upon him was the punishment that made us whole,
      and by his bruises we are healed.
All we like sheep have gone astray;
      we have all turned to our own way,
and the Lord has laid on him
      the iniquity of us all.

He was oppressed, and he was afflicted,
      yet he did not open his mouth;
like a lamb that is led to the slaughter
      and like a sheep that before its shearers is silent,
      so he did not open his mouth.
By a perversion of justice he was taken away.
      Who could have imagined his future?
For he was cut off from the land of the living,
      stricken for the transgression of my people.
They made his grave with the wicked
      and his tomb with the rich,
although he had done no violence,
      and there was no deceit in his mouth.

Yet it was the will of the Lord to crush him with affliction.
When you make his life an offering for sin,
      he shall see his offspring and shall prolong his days;
through him the will of the Lord shall prosper.
      Out of his anguish he shall see;
he shall find satisfaction through his knowledge.
      The righteous one, my servant, shall make many righteous,
      and he shall bear their iniquities.

*Therefore I will allot him a portion with the great,*
*    and he shall divide the spoil with the strong,*
*because he poured out himself to death*
*    and was numbered with the transgressors,*
*yet he bore the sin of many*
*    and made intercession for the transgressors.*
                                        *Isaiah 52:13–53:12*

## Before Your Session

- Carefully read and reread this session's Biblical Foundation. Note words and phrases that attract your attention, and think about what they might mean to you or to others in your group. Write down your questions and try to answer them; you may want to consult trusted Bible commentaries.
- Carefully read chapter 9 of *The Bible With and Without Jesus*. Review the summary for session 4 in the Participant Guide. Note topics about which you want to know more; you may want to consult reputable sources for further information.
- You will need either Bibles for in-person participants or slides prepared with Scripture texts for sharing (identify the translation), or both; newsprint or a markerboard and markers (for in-person sessions); paper, pens or pencils (in-person).
- If using the DVD or streaming video, preview session 4. Choose the best time in your session plan for viewing.

## Starting Your Session

Welcome participants. Discuss:

- What's the most or least helpful thing someone has said *to* you when you were suffering?
- What's the most or least helpful thing *you've* ever said to someone who was suffering?
- When, if ever, has your suffering led to something positive?
- Do you think all suffering happens for a reason? Why or why not?

- Can you think of any occasion when someone suffered on your behalf or you suffered on behalf of another? What are your thoughts about these experiences?

Tell participants that in this session, your group will explore one of the Bible's more challenging considerations of suffering. The passage is difficult not only because of translation issues but also because of its reception history: while it holds a central place in Christianity, it has at best a minor role in Jewish tradition. AJ and Marc suggest the text raises critical questions Jews and Christians can productively ponder together.

## Opening Prayer

*Loving God, as we ponder together the mission of your suffering servant in ancient days, open our eyes to the plight of people suffering now and stir us to help them. Amen.*

## Watch Session Video

Watch the session 4 video together. Discuss:

- What statements in this video most interested, intrigued, surprised, or confused you? Why?
- What questions does this video raise for you?

## "By His Bruises We Are Healed"

Recruit four volunteers to read aloud one of the texts listed below either in the translation from the NRSVue provided here or from their own Bible. You might provide the translations in a handout or on the screen.

> *Be gracious to me, O LORD.*
> *See what I suffer from those who hate me;*
> *you are the one who lifts me up from the gates of death.*
>                                         *Psalm 9:13*

> *The LORD said to the accuser [Hebrew: ha-satan, "the Satan"], "Have you considered my servant Job? There is no one like him on the earth, a blameless*

*and upright man who fears God and turns away from evil." Then the accuser answered the LORD, "Does Job fear God for nothing?... You have blessed the work of his hands, and his possessions have increased in the land. But stretch out your hand now, and touch all that he has, and he will curse you to your face."*

*Job 1:8-11*

*My child, do not despise the LORD's discipline*
*or be weary of his reproof,*
*for the LORD reproves the one he loves,*
*as a father the son in whom he delights.*

*Proverbs 3:11-12*

*Then he [Jesus] began to teach them that the Son of Man must undergo great suffering and be rejected by the elders, the chief priests, and the scribes and be killed and after three days rise again.*

*Mark 8:31*

*Slaves, be subject to your masters with all respect, not only those who are good and gentle but also those who are dishonest. For it is a commendable thing if, being aware of God, a person endures pain while suffering unjustly. If you endure when you are beaten for doing wrong, what credit is that? But if you endure when you do good and suffer for it, this is a commendable thing before God. For to this you have been called, because Christ also suffered for you, leaving you an example, so that you should follow in his steps.*

*1 Peter 2:18-21*

Briefly discuss these questions after each reading:

- What if any value has this suffering?
- Do you think this suffering can be justified?
- Are there times to "suffer in silence" and times to speak up against suffering?
- What if anything has suffering taught you about yourself or about others?

## New Testament Texts

Tell participants that biblical scholars call Isaiah 52:13–53:12 the fourth servant song because it is one of four passages in Second Isaiah

(Isaiah 40–55, composed during the Babylonian Exile) focused on someone identified as God's servant who suffers (the term "suffering servant" does not appear in the Bible, and it is unlikely the passage is a "song" in the sense of something set to music). The New Testament often cites Isaiah 52:13–53:12 in relation to Jesus. When reading Isaiah without the New Testament, however, the identity of the servant "is not self-evident and…there are other candidates for the role" (294).

## The "Suffering Servant" in Historical Context

Have participants turn to Isaiah 52–53. Recruit a volunteer to read aloud 52:13–53:12. Invite participants following in other translations to identify any major differences they noticed.

Discuss:

- What information does the text give about the servant?
- What questions do you have about the servant that the text does not answer?
- Second Isaiah often calls Israel (or synonymously, "Jacob"—Israel's original name, Genesis 32:28) God's "servant" (41:8-9; 44:1-2; 49:3). However, that does not mean that every mention of this servant refers to Israel. What "evidence internal to 52:13–53:12 … suggests that this figure was an individual" (297)? What might identifying the servant as an individual add to your understanding that identifying the servant as a community does not?
- AJ and Marc point out the word for "servant" can be translated "slave." Which translation do you think more appropriate, and why?
- Do you think of yourself as God's servant? As God's slave? Do you think of Moses (Exodus 14:31; Numbers 12:7; NRSVue "servant") or Mary (Luke 1:38; NRSVue "servant"; KJV "handmaid") as God's servant or slave, or both, or neither? What do you make of Paul's identification of the Corinthian congregation as "slaves" (2 Corinthians 4:5)?

- Second Isaiah uses the term "messiah" ("anointed", NRSVue)) once, to refer to Cyrus of Persia (45:1), who conquered Babylon and permitted the peoples Babylon took into exile, including the people of Judah, to return to their homelands. Second Isaiah never mentions an ideal king descended from David—what we term "messiah"; rather, "the covenant promising eternal kingship to David's household is about to be transferred to all Israel" (55:3b-5; 298). What, if anything, do these facts mean for your understanding of this song?

- "The song's death language is figurative, since the passage clearly states that the servant remains alive throughout" (298). What makes death language powerful? Has it become domesticated (for example, "I died laughing", or "that just kills me" or "You're dead to me")? How do literal and metaphorical readings of this language, respectively, shape your understanding of the passage?

- Isaiah 53:10 may refer to "an offering for sin" (NRSVue) or "an offering for guilt" (New Jewish Publication Society [NJPS]; notes in both versions indicate that the meaning of the Hebrew remains uncertain). Can you tease out the different implications of these translations? How can someone's guilt either lead to or cause, or both, someone else's suffering? How can someone's suffering remove the guilt of another?

- "The servant is so severely disabled, in such dreadful condition [53:3, 5, 7, 10], that people do not want to look at him [53:2]. We should linger at these descriptions, since they force us to look at what we do not want to see. In attending to the details, which the prophet forces upon us, we are brought into his suffering rather than becoming inured to it" (300–301). When have you been forced to pay attention to suffering you would rather not have seen? How did you respond?

- What if anything does the servant's suffering do for others? Do we know if the servant willingly suffers for others' benefit? In what ways may you have you benefited from other people's suffering?

- "The sins of Israel cause the servant to be wounded, but this phrase does not state that the wounding is designed to atone. It is a symptom, not a salvation" (301). Has the (unjust) suffering or death of anyone today caused you to reflect on matters of politics or economics? How is unjust, undeserved suffering (53:8) symptomatic of communal sins? How do you respond to such suffering?

# The Servant's History in Jewish and Christian Traditions

Discuss:

- Some rabbinic interpreters identify the suffering servant as the messiah (not as Jesus). For example, *b. Sanhedrin* 98b identifies the messiah as one "we did esteem as one suffering from leprosy" who bandages his sores one by one rather than all at once "because he might be needed at any time and would not want to be delayed." What ethical implications might you draw from the idea that the messiah "may be found among the ones who suffer" (307)?

- In *Pesiqta Rabbati* (fifth to sixth centuries CE), the Messiah ben Ephraim—one of two messiahs, expected to precede the Messiah ben David—willingly takes on seven years of vicarious suffering (though not tied to Isaiah's suffering servant) "with a joyful soul and a glad heart, provided that not one [person] in Israel perish" (307–308). When and how, if ever, has someone willingly suffered for your sake? What effect did their suffering have on you? For whom have you or would you suffer "with a joyful soul and a glad heart," and why?

- Interpreting Isaiah 53:10, one talmudic source (*b. Berakhot* 5a) states that God "may afflict with disease anyone 'in whom the Lord delights.'" AJ and Marc note, "The claim does not glorify suffering. Rather, it suggests that suffering is not arbitrary, that suffering may reflect divine love (see already Prov 3:12), is to be accepted with love for God, and that rabbis too suffer" (309). Can we discern when and whether suffering is God's will? Or, do you think suffering is *never* divine will?

- Marc and AJ insist, "It is inappropriate to suggest... that the Shoah (Holocaust) was ultimately a good thing since it contributed to the existence of the modern State of Israel. The end does not justify the means" (311). How do we prevent the affirmation that God understands suffering, which gives it some value and meaning, without justifying horrific suffering?

## Call to Action

Ask this question from Sister Mary Frances Reis: "Where is the suffering servant to be found today?" (quoted on 312). Lead participants in brainstorming a list of whom they see suffering unjustly, and whose suffering calls for a return to righteousness and justice.

Encourage participants to commit to taking action that alleviates this suffering. Encourage them to choose a first step, not a final step—one that can and will lead to further steps. Invite volunteers to share what action(s) they plan to take.

## Closing Prayer

*You weep, O God, with those who weep, and suffer with those who suffer. You bring hope out of despair, light out of darkness, and life out of death. Strengthen your people to speak for, stand with, and support those who are afflicted, that with them we may see your justice and righteousness, not only in days to come but also today. Hastily bring forth the day when suffering ceases from this world. Amen.*

# SESSION 5

# The Sign of Jonah

## Session Goals

This session's readings, discussion, and reflection will help participants:

- enjoy hearing and telling the story of Jonah,
- explore the story of Jonah in its original historical context while considering ethical questions it raises for today,
- understand how some New Testament authors reread Jonah's story in light of their convictions about Jesus, and
- consider selections of later Christian and Jewish interpretations of Jonah.

## Biblical Foundations

*The sailors said to one another, "Come, let us cast lots, so that we may know on whose account this calamity has come upon us." So they cast lots, and the lot fell on Jonah. Then they said to him, "Tell us why this calamity has come upon us. What is your occupation? Where do you come from? What is your country? And of what people are you?" "I am a Hebrew," he replied. "I worship the LORD, the God of heaven, who made the sea and the dry land."...*

*Then they cried out to the LORD, "Please, O LORD, we pray, do not let us perish on account of this man's life. Do not make us guilty of innocent blood, for you, O LORD, have done as it pleased you." So they picked Jonah up and threw him into the sea, and the sea ceased from its raging. Then the men feared the LORD even more, and they offered a sacrifice to the LORD and made vows.*

*But the LORD provided a large fish to swallow up Jonah, and Jonah was in the belly of the fish three days and three nights.*

*Jonah 1:7-9, 14-17*

*Who is a God like you, pardoning iniquity*
*and passing over the transgression*
*of the remnant of his possession?*
*He does not retain his anger forever*
*because he delights in showing steadfast love.*
*He will again have compassion upon us;*
*he will tread our iniquities under foot.*
*You will cast all our sins*
*into the depths of the sea.*
*You will show faithfulness to Jacob*
*and steadfast love to Abraham,*
*as you have sworn to our ancestors*
*from the days of old.*

*Micah 7:18-20*

# Before Your Session

- Carefully read and reread the Book of Jonah and this session's Biblical Foundations. Note words and phrases that attract your attention, and think about what they might mean to you or to others in your group. Write down your questions and try to answer them; you may want to consult trusted Bible commentaries.

- Carefully read chapter 10 of *The Bible With and Without Jesus*. Review the summary for session 5 in the Participant Guide. Note topics about which you want to know more; you may want to consult reputable sources for further information.

- You will need either Bibles for in-person participants or slides prepared with Scripture texts for sharing (identify the translation), or both; newsprint or a markerboard and markers (for in-person sessions); paper, pens or pencils (in-person).

- If using the DVD or streaming video, preview session 5. Choose the best time in your session plan for viewing.

- *Optional*: Gather several examples of visual art depicting events from Jonah, especially Jonah and the great fish. Choose pieces from a variety of time periods, sources (religious and otherwise), and cultures. Find art online, in illustrated Bibles, in art books, and religious education materials. You may also want to consider children's Bibles.

## Starting Your Session

Welcome participants. Lead participants in brainstorming a list of what they remember about the Book of Jonah. See how much of what they remember is explicit in the text, and what is explicit that they have elided. Write responses on newsprint or markerboard.

*Optional*: Display the artwork you collected. Invite participants to comment on which ones appeal to them most and least, and why? What details, if any, do they think go beyond the Bible's story? What new insights into or questions does the art prompt?

Discuss:

- Do you think the story of Jonah is factual history? Why or why not? On what is your decision based?
- When, if ever, can and should people ask if a biblical text is "necessarily so"? Why?
- AJ and Marc state that "fiction...is often a better teacher than nonfiction." When, if at all, have you experienced fiction's ability to teach?

Read aloud from *The Bible With and Without Jesus*: "Although the historicity of the story [of Jonah] 'ain't necessarily so,' its literary value is superb and its ethical lessons essential" (316). Tell participants your group will explore these aspects of Jonah, and what they may mean for people today.

## Opening Prayer

*Lord God of Israel, who made the sea and the dry land: Where could we escape your spirit, or where could we go to flee your presence? All that has breath is always before you, from the largest fish in the deep to the smallest worm in the soil, and your sovereign will encompasses the mightiest empires and each person's heart. May your word come to us in new ways as we read this ancient story. Amen.*

## Watch Session Video

Watch the session 5 video together. Discuss:

- What statements in this video most interested, intrigued, surprised, or confused you? Why?
- What questions does this video raise for you?

## The Story of Jonah

Recruit volunteers to read aloud Jonah (it should only take around ten minutes). Assign roles to different readers: Jonah, God, the sea captain and his crew, the king of Nineveh—maybe even livestock to make appropriate noise at 3:8! Encourage participants to read in exaggerated ways. (Consider recruiting readers ahead of time, so they can practice.)

After the reading, discuss:

- Many biblical prophets, like Moses and Jeremiah, initially resist their divine commission. How does Jonah resist? Why? If you were called by God, would you resist?
- "Tarshish" has often been understood as a city in Spain, but it may connote "far away." When or where have you "been to Tarshish" —someplace you have gone or something you have done to avoid doing what God is calling you to do? What others have called you to do? What happened?
- In what ways do the ship's captain and sailors prove more faithful to "the LORD [YHWH], the God of heaven" (1:9) than Jonah, who proclaims himself a worshipper (and, in the Septuagint, a servant) of God? Have you ever encountered someone outside your community (religious, national, ethnic) who was more "faithful" to your tradition than you?
- Jonah tells the sailors, "I fear the LORD," though most translations read "worship" (1:9). Which translation do you think is more

appropriate, and why? "Fear God" is frequent biblical counsel
(Deuteronomy 10:12; Psalm 33:8; Matthew 10:28; 2 Corinthians
7:1, etc.). Do you think God is to be "feared" in the sense of to be
afraid of? How do such images fit with the view of a loving and
merciful God?

- "Jonah, the epitome of a passive-aggressive personality, knows
  that he has caused the problem [for the sailors], but he refuses to
  take responsibility for fixing it" (324). Do you agree with AJ and
  Marc's characterization of Jonah? Do you "like" Jonah (would you
  have coffee with him)? Do you see him as role model, negative
  exemplar, both, or neither?

- Among the questions Jonah 1 raises, AJ and Marc write, are, "Do
  we kill one person for the good of the many?...Or, do we take
  the chance that working together we might all survive?" (324).
  How do you assess Jonah's plan of throwing him overboard? When
  might you have taken a chance of working with others for a positive
  outcome? What happened?

- What do you make of Jonah's prayer in the belly of the fish? Do you
  think it is "self-serving" as AJ and Marc state (325), or sincere—or
  a bit of each?

- "With . . . references to rescue from Sheol," Jonah's prayer "prompts
  readers to think about what it means to be alive to the world,
  its possibilities and promises" (326). When was a time you, like
  Jonah, received a second chance? What did you do with it?

- Jonah "was hoping to experience *schadenfreude*. He wanted the
  evil people to be punished rather than given a second chance"
  (328). Can you identify with Jonah's great anger? Have you
  ever experienced *schadenfreude*, taking pleasure at the misery of
  someone else? How did this experience make you feel?

- Jonah's second prayer (4:2-3, "I knew that you are a gracious
  and merciful God, slow to anger, abounding in steadfast love,
  and relenting from punishment") identifies defining attributes of
  Israel's God (compare Exodus 20:5-6; 34:6-7; Deuteronomy 5:9-
  10), although he omits God's promise to "by no means [clear] the

guilty." Is it fair to abbreviate a biblical text in this way? What problems can arise when we ignore God's justice at the expense of God's mercy, or vice versa? What makes justice without mercy as "intolerable" (329) as mercy without justice?

- In 722 BCE, the Assyrian Empire destroyed the Northern Kingdom of Israel. "The repentant one day may be the sinful the next; we all have the potential both to repent and to ravage" (330). How does knowing Assyria's place in Israel's history affect your understanding of Jonah's story?

- God expresses concern and compassion also for Nineveh's "many animals" (4:11)—in fact, the final words of the books are "and also many animals." What ethical implications, if any, does God's care for animals have for our own?

## The Gospels and the Sign of Jonah

Explain that in Mark, probably the earliest Gospel, Jesus asks, "Why does this generation ask for a sign? Truly I tell you, no sign will be given to this generation" (8:12). In Matthew 12:38-42 and Luke 11:29-32, Jesus mentions a cryptic sign.

Have half the class read Matthew 12:38-42 ("Then some of the scribes and Pharisees said to him, 'Teacher, we wish to see a sign from you.' But he answered them, 'An evil and adulterous generation asks for a sign, but no sign will be given to it except the sign of the prophet Jonah. For just as Jonah was three days and three nights in the belly of the sea monster, so for three days and three nights the Son of Man will be in the heart of the earth. The people of Nineveh will rise up at the judgment with this generation and condemn it, because they repented at the proclamation of Jonah, and indeed something greater than Jonah is here! The queen of the South will rise up at the judgment with this generation and condemn it, because she came from the ends of the earth to listen to the wisdom of Solomon, and indeed something greater than Solomon is here!'") and have them note what they think the "sign of Jonah" means.

Have the other half of the class read Luke 11:29-32 ("When the crowds were increasing, he began to say, 'This generation is an evil generation; it asks for a sign, but no sign will be given to it except the sign of Jonah. For just as Jonah became a sign to the people of Nineveh, so the Son of Man will be to this generation. The queen of the South will rise at the judgment with the people of this generation and condemn them, because she came from the ends of the earth to listen to the wisdom of Solomon, and indeed, something greater than Solomon is here! The people of Nineveh will rise up at the judgment with this generation and condemn it, because they repented at the proclamation of Jonah, and indeed, something greater than Jonah is here!'") and similarly have them note what they think the "sign of Jonah" means.

Discuss:

- Who asks Jesus for a sign? Why do you think they ask? Why do you think is Jesus reluctant to offer one? What do you think the sign in each story signifies?
- Read Mark 4:35-41, the story of Jesus asleep in a boat during the storm. How might knowing that this story is a parody of Jonah's story affect your interpretation and appreciation of it?

## Jonah in Christian and Jewish Eyes

Discuss:

- Saint Jerome sees Jonah as prefiguring Jesus because both "leave their home of safety and descend into the world of sin" (334). How convincing do you find this allegorical connection, and why?
- Martin Luther said the Book of Jonah represented "Judaism's envy and jealousy" of Christianity: "In Luther's works and many others, Jonah is a representative both of the Christ and of the faults and the fall of the Jews and Judaism" (335). How is this view a misreading? How can regarding Jonah as an "antihero" not to be emulated guard against anti-Jewish readings?

- In the deuterocanonical/apocryphal Book of Tobit, Tobit and his son Tobias rejoice over the destruction of Nineveh (in 612 BCE). How do you assess biblical texts, or news reports, that celebrate a people's destruction? Under what circumstances, if any, should destruction of a location and its inhabitants be celebrated?

- Jewish interpreters expanded on details on Nineveh's repentance— for example, by depicting the residents tearing down the royal palace and returning individual stolen bricks to their rightful owners, or by unraveling garments to return stolen threads (see 339–340). What is the greatest length to which you've gone to make amends, and how was your action received? Should there be a limit to such amends?

- "Medieval Jewish commentators go out of their way to celebrate the righteousness of the sailors—a far cry from Luther's perception that the book is narrowly nationalistic" (341). When have you witnessed righteous individuals outside your own community? Do you, or does your community, celebrate the good works of outsiders?

- Jewish congregations hear the Book of Jonah on the afternoon of Yom Kippur, the Day of Atonement, "the most sacred of Jewish days. . . . The connection of Jonah to Yom Kippur is the book's concern for repentance: even the most wicked, if they sincerely repent, will be forgiven" (337–338). If you are outside the Jewish tradition, when (if ever) have you heard the entire Book of Jonah or passages of it read in a worship context?

## Call to Action

Close your session by asking participants to discuss one of these questions, sparked by questions AJ and Marc raise:

- What sort of God do we want: "the one who forgives or the one who destroys" (329)? What does our answer mean for the way we should live?

- "What are we called to do, and how do we follow difficult callings, even those that call on us to engage positively with our enemies?" (343)
- "The book of Jonah insists that life has meaning"—human life, animal life, plant life (343). What are we doing to honor all life?

# Closing Prayer

Tell participants many Jewish congregations read Micah 7:18-20 on Yom Kippur after the Book of Jonah. Read those verses aloud together as this session's Closing Prayer:

> Who is a God like you, pardoning iniquity
>> and passing over the transgression
>> of the remnant of his possession?
> He does not retain his anger forever
>> because he delights in showing steadfast love.
> He will again have compassion upon us;
>> he will tread our iniquities under foot.
> You will cast all our sins
>> into the depths of the sea.
> You will show faithfulness to Jacob
>> and steadfast love to Abraham,
> as you have sworn to our ancestors
>> from the days of old.

# SESSION 6

# "My God, My God, Why Have You Forsaken Me?"

## Session Goals

This session's readings, discussion, and reflection will help participants:

- read Psalm 22 in its original historical context,
- understand how and why the Gospel writers draw on Psalm 22 in their accounts of Jesus's crucifixion,
- appreciate several later Jewish interpretations of Psalm 22, and
- consider the place of lament in their own prayer.

## Biblical Foundation

*My God, my God, why have you forsaken me?*
    *Why are you so far from helping me, from the words of my groaning?*
*O my God, I cry by day, but you do not answer;*
    *and by night but find no rest.*

*Yet you are holy,*
    *enthroned on the praises of Israel.*
*In you our ancestors trusted;*
    *they trusted, and you delivered them.*
*To you they cried and were saved;*
    *in you they trusted and were not put to shame.*

*But I am a worm and not human,*
    *scorned by others and despised by the people.*
*All who see me mock me;*
    *they sneer at me; they shake their heads;*

*"Commit your cause to the LORD; let him deliver—*
    *let him rescue the one in whom he delights!"*

*Yet it was you who took me from the womb;*
    *you kept me safe on my mother's breast.*
*On you I was cast from my birth,*
    *and since my mother bore me you have been my God.*
*Do not be far from me,*
    *for trouble is near,*
    *and there is no one to help.*

*Many bulls encircle me;*
    *strong bulls of Bashan surround me;*
*they open wide their mouths at me,*
    *like a ravening and roaring lion.*

*I am poured out like water,*
    *and all my bones are out of joint;*
*my heart is like wax;*
    *it is melted within my breast;*
*my mouth is dried up like a potsherd,*
    *and my tongue sticks to my jaws;*
    *you lay me in the dust of death.*

*For dogs are all around me;*
    *a company of evildoers encircles me;*
*they bound my hands and feet.*
*I can count all my bones.*
*They stare and gloat over me;*
*they divide my clothes among themselves,*
    *and for my clothing they cast lots.*

*But you, O LORD, do not be far away!*
    *O my help, come quickly to my aid!*
*Deliver my soul from the sword,*
    *my life from the power of the dog!*
*Save me from the mouth of the lion!*

*From the horns of the wild oxen you have rescued me.*
*I will tell of your name to my brothers and sisters;*
    *in the midst of the congregation I will praise you:*

*You who fear the Lord, praise him!*
    *All you offspring of Jacob, glorify him;*
        *stand in awe of him, all you offspring of Israel!*
*For he did not despise or abhor*
        *the affliction of the afflicted;*
*he did not hide his face from me*
        *but heard when I cried to him.*

*From you comes my praise in the great congregation;*
        *my vows I will pay before those who fear him.*
*The poor shall eat and be satisfied;*
        *those who seek him shall praise the LORD.*
        *May your hearts live forever!*

*All the ends of the earth shall remember*
        *and turn to the LORD,*
*and all the families of the nations*
        *shall worship before him.*
*For dominion belongs to the LORD,*
        *and he rules over the nations.*

*To him, indeed, shall all who sleep in the earth bow down;*
        *before him shall bow all who go down to the dust,*
        *and I shall live for him.*
*Posterity will serve him;*
        *future generations will be told about the Lord*
*and proclaim his deliverance to a people yet unborn,*
        *saying that he has done it.*

                                                    *Psalm 22*

# Before Your Session

- Carefully read and reread this session's Biblical Foundation. Note words and phrases that attract your attention, and think about what they might mean to you or to others in your group. Write down your questions and try to answer them; you may want to consult trusted Bible commentaries.

- Carefully read chapter 11 of *The Bible With and Without Jesus*. Review the summary for session 6 in the Participant Guide. Note topics about which you want to know more; you may want to consult reputable sources for further information.

- You will need either Bibles for in-person participants or slides prepared with Scripture texts for sharing (identify the translation), or both; newsprint or a markerboard and markers (for in-person sessions); paper, pens or pencils (in-person).

- If using the DVD or streaming video, preview session 6. Choose the best time in your session plan for viewing.

## Starting Your Session

Welcome participants. Lead them in brainstorming their view of *lament*: when have they ever lamented, or complained, to God, to others, to themselves?

Over what did they lament: a missed opportunity, a decision that proved to be wrong, the cancellation of a favorite television show; the defeat of a team; a change in leadership in a religious institution, company, political office; the loss of a loved one, and so forth.

What forms did this lament take: crying, silence, praying, screaming, moping?

Did voicing the problem help resolve the issue?

## Opening Prayer

*O God, you call us to pray with our whole selves—heart and mind, strength and spirit, breath and voice. May this study equip us better to relate to you in grief and in gladness, in sorrow and in celebration. Amen.*

## Watch Session Video

Watch the session 6 video segment together. Discuss:

- What statements in this video most interested, intrigued, surprised, or confused you? Why?

- What questions does this video segment raise for you?

## Psalm 22 in the Scriptures of Israel

Tell participants the Book of Psalms, though traditionally attributed to King David, is "a compilation of liturgical poetry from many periods and by many authors" (358), much as a hymnal can contain hymns from different times and hands. Although Jews and Christians, by and large, share the psalter, they interpret some of the same psalms very differently, including Psalm 22.

Remind participants that most Christians are familiar with the first verse of Psalm 22, because Mark and Matthew say Jesus cried its first words from his cross. However, not all Christians realize Jesus is quoting a psalm. As AJ and Marc explain, the Gospels connect many details from Psalm 22 to Jesus's crucifixion. Therefore, the more one knows about the Scriptures of Israel, the better one can appreciate the New Testament.

Explain that while for Christians, the psalm is intimately and inextricably connected to Jesus, it has additional value, for the meaning of Scripture is inexhaustible. Jesus was not, and need not be, the only person who felt that Psalm 22 spoke to personal circumstances.

Recruit three volunteers to read Psalm 22 aloud (from different translations, if possible): 22:1-11; 22:12-21; and 22:22-31. After the reading, discuss:

- Under what circumstances might you imagine this psalm could have been recited in ancient Israel?
- "Because many of the psalmists of lament are convinced of their own innocence, their psalms can be understood as protest literature that addresses the problem of theodicy, the justice of God" (363). How (if you do) do you think about God's justice and goodness in the face of unjust suffering?
- "Although present-day worshippers might consider it impolite to issue commands to God, ancient Israel did not" (363). What commands does the psalmist issue to God? Have you ever used the imperative in relation to God (Christian participants might consider the "Our Father" prayer)? Why do you think the psalmist

argues that God should pay attention? Do you consider these commands "impolite"?

- "Unlike many laments, this psalm does not call for vengeance or for a curse against the enemies" (365). What significance, if any, do you find in this difference? Do you find asking for God to take vengeance against enemies a helpful prayer since vengeance belongs to God (Deuteronomy 32:35; Romans 12:19; Hebrews 10:30), or do you find the idea of vengeance in general repugnant? What do you think the difference is between vengeance and justice, or justified punishment?
- How like or unlike your own prayers is Psalm 22? How often or freely do you complain or lament to God? Why?

## Jesus and Psalm 22

The Gospels draw several connections between Psalm 22 and the Crucifixion, and each opens questions for consideration. Connections you and the participants may want to consider include the following.

Psalm 22:1 reads "My God, my God, why have you forsaken me? / Why are you so far from helping me, from the words of my groaning?" (cited in Mark 15:34 and Matthew 27:46)

- How does knowing the rest of the psalm influence your understanding of Jesus's cry?
- Why do you think Luke and John omit this cry?
- Is the cry consistent with John's assertion that Jesus and the Father "are one" (John 10:30).

The Hebrew for "my God" is "Eli"—which sounds very much like the Hebrew name of the prophet Elijah. Matthew 27:47 and Mark 15:35 depict people thinking that Jesus is calling Elijah. Read Malachi 4:5 ("See, I will send you the prophet Elijah before the great and terrible day of the LORD comes").

- Might Jesus have called Elijah?

- Have you ever wished for the end of the world?
- If you knew the world was about to end, what would you say? What would you do?

Psalm 22:18 states, "They divide my clothes among themselves, / and for my clothing they cast lots."

- Matthew 27:35; Mark 15:24; Luke 23:34; John 19:24 report that the Roman soldiers cast lots for Jesus's clothing. Why do you think all four Gospels include this seemingly minor detail?
- Do you think the parallels between the accounts of Jesus's crucifixion and Psalm 22 are the result of the Gospels recording what actually happened? Or, do you think they are examples of the New Testament's "tendency...to use the 'Old Testament' as a template for telling the story of Jesus" (351)? Both? Neither? Why? In what ways if any does the answer matter for how you understand the Gospel?

Psalm 22 concludes (verses 28-31):

*For dominion belongs to the LORD,*
  *and he rules over the nations.*

*To him, indeed, shall all who sleep in the earth bow down;*
  *before him shall bow all who go down to the dust,*
  *and I shall live for him.*
*Posterity will serve him;*
  *future generations will be told about the Lord*
*and proclaim his deliverance to a people yet unborn,*
  *saying that he has done it.*

- Does knowing how the psalm ends change the way you initially assessed the opening verse?

## Psalm 22 in Jewish Sources

Read aloud Marc and AJ's comment: "The earliest rabbinic sources rarely cite Psalm 22; perhaps the rabbis ignored it because it was so significant to early Christians" (371). When they do cite the psalm, Jewish sources see it referring to Queen Esther, King David (whom the superscription names as author), a messianic figure other than Jesus, the Jewish people collectively, and others.

Discuss:

- The Septuagint (Greek) version of Esther contains several sections absent in the Hebrew version; in one of these, "Esther prays using language likely taken from Psalm 22" (372), and the Babylonian Talmud associates Psalm 22 with Esther's prayer (373–374). Does the psalm take on new meaning if you associate it with figures other than Jesus?

- *Pesiqta Rabbati* presents Psalm 22 as the lament of the Messiah ben Ephraim, "a messianic figure who precedes the main Davidic messiah and, according to a few rabbinic texts, dies a martyr" (375; see also session 4). Read AJ and Marc's summary of this narrative (375–376). What might the story mean on its own, and as a reflection of polemics between Jews and Christians?

- Several medieval Jewish interpreters regard the singular speaker in Psalm 22 as "concerning the entire nation of Israel together, for they are like one person in exile, with one heart" (Kimchi, quoted on 377). How does this corporate interpretation affect your understanding of Psalm 22? How is this related to the common Jewish idea that the suffering servant represents all Israel? Do you see problems, or possibilities, in placing the psalm on the lips of people other than Jesus? Would you be comfortable praying this psalm for yourself?

## Call to Action

Read aloud from *The Bible With and Without Jesus*: "The psalm speaks to horror and danger, but it speaks to more than that. It allows us to express the feeling that many of us have had—that God has abandoned us. At the same time, it ironically insists that we have not abandoned that relationship.

A lament psalm is a poem of raw honesty and fidelity. It is appropriate on the lips of Jesus the Jew, and anyone who feels abandoned by God" (379).

Invite participants to write their own laments—using whatever language comes naturally to them. If they do not currently need to lament, invite them to remember a time they did—or to compose a lament for any situation of unjust suffering.

Thank participants for studying *The Bible With and Without Jesus* with you. Discuss:

- How has this study affected the way you read any of the Bible passages considered?
- What insight have you gained from the study?
- What questions do you still have? How will you go about answering them?

## Closing Prayer

*We thank you, gracious God, for this opportunity to read and reflect on Scripture together. We praise you for continuing to guide us toward the righteous and holy lives for which you created us. Amen.*

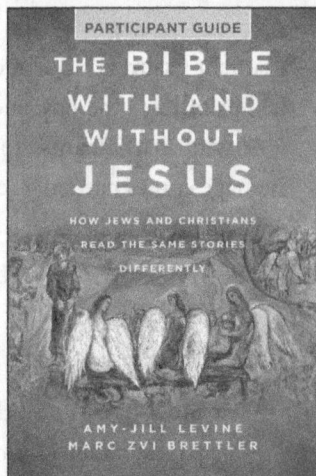

www.ingramcontent.com/pod-product-compliance
Lightning Source LLC
LaVergne TN
LVHW031227120425
808384LV00004B/7